world trade center
the giants that defied the sky

CONTENTS

world tra

te center

TEXTS BY
PETER SKINNER

EDITORIAL PROJECT
VALERIA MANFERTO DE FABIANIS

GRAPHIC DESIGN
PATRIZIA BALOCCO LOVISETTI

© 2002 White Star S.r.l.
Via C. Sassone, 24 - 13100 Vercelli, Italy - www.whitestar.it
New up-dated edition

This edition published by
Barnes & Noble, Inc., by arrangement with White Star S.r.l.
2003 Barnes & Noble Books

ISBN 0-7607-4690-7
M10987654321

Library of Congress
Cataloging-in-Publication
Data available

Printed in Italy by Rotolito Lombarda - Color separation: Fotomec

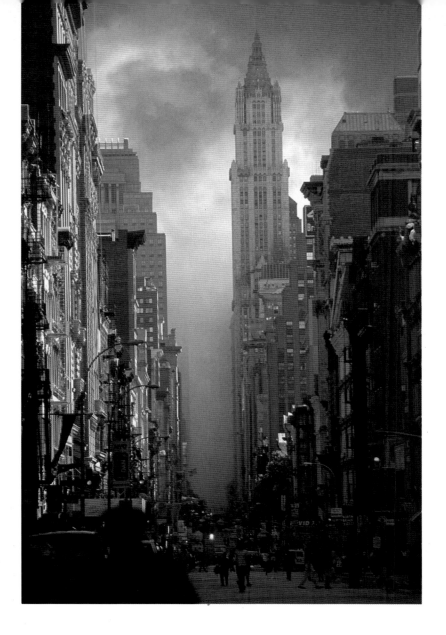

PREFACE

BY MIKE WALLACE

The hijacked planes that zeroed in on New York and Washington with such murderous accuracy obviously chose their targets for a reason. They didn't attack Los Angeles and Miami, after all. Why not? It's reasonable to assume that they chose cities and buildings that they believed had great symbolic and actual potency: the respective headquarters of the military and financial institutions whose decisions have tremendous impact throughout the globe.

As we've seen from the outpouring of support from around the world, millions of people love and admire the United States and its pre-eminent urban centers.

But others hate us passionately. Not, despite what some say, because we are the land of the free and good, but because the nation has embraced policies from which they feel they've suffered. Driven by calculated strategy and suicidal fanaticism, they've dealt a terrific blow to proud towers and command centers alike.

New Yorkers are rolling with the blow magnificently, despite the added shock of having it come both figuratively and literally out of the clear blue sky, shattering our sense of invulnerability. But that sense always rested on a truncated reading of history. While the particular form of the attack was fiendishly novel, New York, over nearly four centuries, has repeatedly been the object of murderous intentions. Through a combination of luck and power, we have escaped many of the intended blows, but not all of them, and our forebears often feared that worse might yet befall them.

In recent decades, some opponents of the expanding global cultural and economic order of which New York and Washington were seen as headquarters, turned to terror. The resulting mayhem seldom touched New York's shores—the first World Trade Center attack was a notable exception—but fantasies about urban destruction exploded in popular culture. The popularity of cinematic depictions of overseas (or alien) predators wreaking havoc on New York and Washington, with the World Trade Center and Statue of Liberty as attendant casualties, was perhaps also fueled by antagonism to Big Government and Big Corporations.

Now these fantasies have been horribly realized—one reason that we've repeatedly heard stunned witnesses exclaiming the devastation seemed "unreal" or "just like a movie." This is not to say that terrorists are copycats and that Hollywood's to blame, but rather that cultural producers, like almost everyone else, tend to assume that New York and Washington are the likeliest targets.

One consequence of reality having caught up to fiction might be a new reluctance to spin such fantasies—a reissue of "Independence Day" was just postponed—though it's equally likely that someone is already hard at work on a mini-series.

More hopefully, our shattered sense of invulnerability will be replaced by a sober appreciation of the fact that, even as we mourn our casualties, take prudent precautions to prevent similar attacks, help track down and punish those responsible, and reconstruct our city, our generation of New Yorkers, like those that preceded ours, has witnessed and survived a cataclysm even worse than our imaginations had been able to conceive.

17
The twin Towers frame the
Woolworth Building (1913),
"The Cathedral of Commerce"
designed by Gilbert Cass. To the right
is 1 World Financial Center.

N ew York!
The fabled city with the
dramatic skyline, beacon for
the best and the brightest,
for the fortune seeker, the
immigrant—for anyone in
search of opportunity. But
New York is young and has to
create its own myths. New
York does this superbly—and
believes absolutely in its own
grandiose projections. New
Yorkers' lives are shaped by
images: they are convinced
the city offers the newest,

city was booming; the future
was bright and beckoning.

Too easily New York forgets
past crises—even though
their causes and results live
on. In retrospect they seem
less acute; in fact they are
more numerous and serious
than New Yorkers want to
admit. The race antagonisms
that blew up in the mid-
1960s, the near-bankruptcy
that sandbagged New York in
the mid-1970s, the inadequate
performance of the public

casing the cocktail party
crowd, bouncing from affaire
to affaire with an army of
trainers and therapists to
provide physical and
psychological makeovers as
needed. Tomorrow was never
just another day; it was a
bigger, better opportunity.
There would be another
model being photographed in
the park, another film-shoot
in process on the block. New
friends and new relationships
beckoned by the minute. If

INTRODUCTION

the smartest, and the coolest.
They speak in superlatives,
sure that New York is the
biggest and the best; its ideas
and products shape the
world—and the world
persuades them this is true.

The Twin Towers silently
voiced it all. They caught and
reflected the city's optimism
and energy. Though massive,
they were lean and clean
enough in proportion and
style to win general
acceptance. Leave the
pinnacles and spires and
filigreed elegance to older
cities; New York projects
power and purpose. By 1980,
everyone had forgotten that
the World Trade Center had
been a hotly debated project,
that during the 1960s
construction had been a slow,
disruptive process, and that in
the 1970s renting the new
space had been difficult. That
was the past; New York lived
in the present, dreaming of
the future. In the 1990s the

schools, the spiraling costs of
housing, the lack of entry-
level jobs, the increasing gap
between rich and poor, and
the city's slow strangulation
by traffic—all persist. As for
other big-city ills such as
noise, dirt, poor air quality
and incomprehensible
tongues, New Yorkers simply
take them for granted. "This
is New York—the world's
most exciting city. Whatever
the problems, we can fix
them," they persuade
themselves. New Yorkers live
for the new: the new job, the
new apartment, lover,
vacation, restaurant, show,
movie, book. The economy
and the city seem endlessly
inventive; while one bubble
burst, the next confidently
swelled. New York could
never be truly at risk.

The young professionals
seem peerless and fearless;
well-paid, well-groomed,
ascending the corporate
escalator, closing the deals,

life in London, Paris, Rome,
Istanbul, New Delhi, Hong
Kong and another half-dozen
great cities was just as
sophisticated and exciting as
in New York, so what! New
Yorkers discounted the claim.
It had to be better here: this
is New York!

But myth and reality and
symbol and substance were
beginning to separate even
before the brilliant, sunny
morning of September 11,
2001. The dot.com world was
deflating like a punctured
balloon. People who normally
vacationed in Europe
announced sudden, urgent
needs to visit their parents in
the Mid-West. The thin,
nervy models were a little
thinner and considerably
more nervy, and the film-
shoots on the streets served
their crews bagels and cream
cheese rather than brioches
and imported jams. But New
York still held reality at bay;
this was merely a temporary

18 AND 19
THE MOMENT OF IMPACT—FOR THE
NORTH TOWER 8:45 A.M. AND FOR THE
SOUTH TOWER 9:03 A.M.—MEANT A
DELUGE OF 20,000 GALLONS OF JET FUEL
FLOODING IN, BURSTING INTO FLAMES
AND CREATING A TEMPERATURE IN EXCESS
OF 2,000°F.

20-21
FROM DULL BRONZE TO GLEAMING GOLD.
THE TWIN TOWERS' ANODIZED ALUMINUM
SKIN PROVED REMARKABLY SENSITIVE TO
EXTERNAL LIGHT CONDITIONS, DAY BY DAY,
SEASON BY SEASON.

22-23
A CATASTROPHE BEYOND BELIEF CREATES
UNFORGETTABLE IMAGES OF DEATH AND
DESTRUCTION.

economic downturn, a useful correction; the system was shaking out the fat, tensing up for the next forward surge. Real trouble occurred only elsewhere; horrific events in Rwanda, in Serbia, in Bosnia and Kosovo; the frequent flare-ups in the Israel-Palestine confrontation and the occasional flare-ups in Northern Ireland were far away, almost unreal.

America remained blessed, beyond the reach of wars and shootings in the streets; Americans didn't have to listen to the day's death toll each evening on the TV news.

What New York and America lost on September 11, 2001 was not only thousands of innocent lives tragically ended, great buildings reduced to rubble and vibrant businesses blasted into bankruptcy. New York and America lost the deeply held myth of some peculiar, sacrosanct core of invincibility. Defying the horrific events of its own recent history, America had clung to this myth. New Yorkers managed to filter experience: the 1993 World Trade Center bombing had not brought the tower down; in the fullness of time the perpetrators were brought to justice.

The 1997 Oklahoma bombing was far more lethal, with 138 victims compared to six in the WTC bombing, but America assured itself this was a uniquely aberrational domestic crime, perpetrated by an American. The nation's mistake was to concentrate on the trials and the punishments of the perpetrators; the crime was to neglect the evidence of American vulnerability. In retrospect, it is clear that in September 2001 the intelligence and security systems maintained to protect New York and its bridges, tunnels, transportation, electrical and water supply were utterly inadequate.

Just what precautions can be taken and at what cost to a democratic nation's open society and civil liberties is hard to define. It would be easy enough in Tokyo, Beijing, Cairo or Riyadh to "keep an eye on foreigners" because they are so few and so identifiable. It's a different situation in European capitals with their broader mix of residents, and an even more different situation in major American cities, which have thoroughly mixed populations and remarkably few restrictions on activities or movement. Diversity and freedom are the blood and oxygen of American life.

On September 11, every American and most of the world's citizens realized an era had ended and life would thereafter be different. The nationwide response after the initial shock and the heroic rescue efforts says much for America. The instant solidarity felt between individuals in their communities and between the American people and their government, the refusal of individual Americans to ostracize Muslims, and the restraint Americans sought and their government has practiced in terms of retaliatory action all speak of great moral strength. The

saving thought is that whatever the suffering now brought to Afghanistan, it will not equal the suffering that the Taliban continues to inflict.

It is a superb irony that many powerful Muslim critics of American government and policy live and work freely and untrammeled in America while in Muslim nations few critics of government remain free and at large for long. It's an irony too that the terrorists thrive only in the hinterlands of the least effectively governed Islamic nations, despised and condemned by thinking citizens. But a stronger, more immediate take on reality is to be found in asking a local Muslim cab driver, shish-kebab cart operator or newsstand owner in New York what he wants most. The answer very seldom has to do with American policy or Islam; it is most often the statement, "To bring the rest of my family to America."

Muslim immigrants willingly accept America with all her challenges. They are not afraid of hard work or raising families or taking on the risks of starting businesses; not afraid of naming their land of birth or practicing their religion. If they are afraid of anything, it is the remote possibility of being forced to return home. Their children move through the public schools and distinguish themselves in the nation's colleges and universities; they become Americans. Now for them and their parents, there is a fear: they may be at risk of death through the actions of their former countrymen who hate the nation that they, the successful immigrants, have come to love.

world tra

CHAPTER

1

MANHATTAN BEFORE
THE TWIN TOWERS

To picture New York and its life before the Twin Towers requires revisiting the 1960s, the decade before the towers were built. They were completed more than thirty years ago; the North Tower's first tenants moved in 1970 and the South Tower's did so in 1971. For a majority of New Yorkers and tristate area residents the Twin Towers have always been there, always visible, a lodestar and an undeniable fact of life. It takes conscious effort of will to conjure up the New York of the 1960s; recapturing the state and texture of the city demands more than just recalling the exuberant youth rebellion, the rock-and-roll highlights and the superficial 'good times glow' of that decade, especially its middle years. It requires searching for the underlying realities: the who-was-who among political leaders, the state of the economy, race relations, public services, education, and housing; it means examining perceptions about crime and public safety, about the quality of life and levels of confidence. For most people under forty the 1960s decade was before their time, ancient history they never shared. For those over sixty, it's "the old days," when life was different, more manageable—a time now slipping away in the haze of overburdened memory.

In 1960 John F. Kennedy was president, Nelson Rockefeller was governor of New York State, and Robert F. Wagner was mayor of New York. They were a trio of big, confident leaders in a big, bold decade. But it was a difficult, demanding decade in which prosperity and an

exuberant youth culture often seemed to be forces designed to keep people's minds off disasters. The Vietnam War and student protest, the assassination of President Kennedy, race riots and cities on fire, and then on to Watergate . . . Yet it remained a surprisingly optimistic decade—and New York did not seem to take its problems too seriously.

New York did not lack for iconic buildings before the Twin Towers soared 1,360 feet up from their Plaza into the heavens. Solid, vibrant Rockefeller Center, largely completed in the 1930s, with its mall and flag-studded sunken Plaza, was a major attraction, awash with New Yorkers and tourists. The city was affectionately proud of the Chrysler and Empire State buildings, both in midtown, rising high above their neighbors to dominate the skyline. The former (completed in 1930 and 1,046 ft high) was famous for its stainless-steel eagle heads, art deco trim and its 71st floor visitors' center; the latter (completed in 1931 and 1,250 ft high) offered an immensely popular observation deck. Both had ideal locations. The Chrysler building is only a block from Grand Central Terminal where the railway network serves the northern suburbs, and the Empire State building is conveniently close to Penn Station, with rail service to Long Island and New Jersey.

These two monumental stations have cautionary histories. Penn Station, modeled on the baths of Caracalla in Rome, was completed in 1911. In 1965, real estate interests

demolished it and built a bland office tower and covered arena. Only an intensely spirited public protest led by Jacqueline Bouvier Kennedy saved the magnificent Grand Central Terminal, completed in 1913 and famed for its vast, barrel-roofed Main Concourse, from a similar fate. Grand Central, now totally restored to its former splendor, is a visitors' "must see" destination, drawing millions annually.

Downtown in Lower Manhattan's Financial District, to the southeast of the Twin Towers' site, the 66-story Woolworth Building ("The Cathedral of Commerce," completed 1913) rose in relative isolation at Broadway and Park Place, a proud architectural icon, admired for its elegant masonry and terracotta cladding. The building looked across at City Hall (1812), a refined, cupola-topped two-story pavilion in a tree-filled park, and just south of it, to the bulkier, recently restored Victorian-classical Tweed Court House (1878). The three buildings are distinguished standouts of fine architecture, though a number of handsome older stone-clad office buildings keep them company. All could afford to be scornful of the banal new office towers plugged into to every possible site, particularly toward Wall Street and the south. To the casual visitor or the fast-moving tourist, New York seemed to be on wave of prosperity, enjoying boom times. The truth was far different; the city was entering stormy financial waters and within a decade would be poised on the brink of bankruptcy.

28-29
GOVERNORS ISLAND (LEFT FOREGROUND), EX-U.S. COAST GUARD HQ, IS AVAILABLE FOR $1 (WITH EXPENSIVE CONDITIONS). MOST OF MANHATTAN'S HUDSON RIVER PASSENGER AND FREIGHT PIERS HAVE BEEN DEMOLISHED, VICTIMS OF RISING COSTS. TOP LEFT: GEORGE WASHINGTON BRIDGE, BOTTOM RIGHT, BROOKLYN BRIDGE, WITH MANHATTAN BRIDGE JUST NORTH. SOUTH OF BROOKLYN BRIDGE IS THE HISTORIC BROOKLYN HEIGHTS RESIDENTIAL AREA.

29
THE LOVER MANHATTAN SKYLINE SEEN THROUGH BROOKLYN BRIDGE'S SUSPENSION CABLES.

A major cause of the city's worsening financial plight was the 1965 federal and state mandate that the city pay 25 percent of its welfare and associated medical care costs, previously entirely met from state and federal sources. Other causes included liberal welfare policies that added recipients to the public assistance rolls and generous pay raises for the city's fast-growing unionized workforce. Between 1960 and 1970, New York's budget more than tripled to over $6 billion. To meet financial needs, the city borrowed money, incurring heavy repayment obligations. By 1971, when the second of the Twin Towers was

30 TOP AND 30-31
New "box" high-rises intrude among older, decorative skyscrapers. Foreground: the 5-bay Staten Island Ferry Terminal—home of the famous "5-cent ride." Mid-left: the circular Castle Clinton (1807) in Battery Park, once guarding New York Harbor.

31 BOTTOM RIGHT
President and Mrs. Kennedy, seen in an open motorcade on Lower Broadway, were warmly welcomed visitors to New York. Ticker-tape parades were reserved for sports victories or foreign heads of state, though in 1960, JFK enjoyed one as a presidential candidate.

completed, the city was headed for financial disaster, with longer term loan repayment costs exceeding its current budget.

No remedies were in sight: property taxes had been hiked to the bearable maximum and new taxes added to business and personal income. As a result, businesses and residents were beginning to leave New York for more welcoming financial climates. Thus the gleaming Twin Towers, with 10 million square feet of brand-new office space, rose over a city is precipitous decline.

Though clear to the well informed, the city's rapidly worsening financial situation remained happily masked to millions of citizens and visitors. "Urban renewal," meaning a building boom, was a catchword; new office towers and apartment buildings were rising. The construction of Lincoln Center for the Performing Arts was underway, projected to be not only a cultural center but also a new anchor and catalyst for economic revival of the West Side between 59th and 72nd streets. Philharmonic Hall

(later renamed Avery Fisher Hall) opened in 1962, New York State Theater in 1964, and the Metropolitan Opera House in 1966. Much emphasis was given to the central Plaza that opened on to these first three Lincoln Center buildings. It was a welcoming public meeting place, a civic amenity, reflecting the marriage of the arts and life. The sight of the Plaza thronged with lively crowds from midday to mid-evening was not lost on the World Trade Center's planners and architects.

Behind the glitter and below the surface, New York was experiencing wrenching strains. The schools were seen as segregated and failing their minority students, and the educational bureaucracy was under heavy fire. "Experimental districts," with control by community school boards with parent participation, had led to a prolonged teacher strike. Concern existed that minorities were denied access to higher education, and in 1970 the city college system adopted a much criticized "open admissions" policy.

The Vietnam War had led to increasingly tense and disruptive demonstrations, and in 1968, student riots broke out at Columbia University over the university's collaboration with the Institute of Defense Analysis and its lack of support for community development in neighboring Harlem.

As the 1960s closed, the city was visibly in decline. The economy was weakening, public services were being cut, and the subways and commuter railroads were deteriorating. New York was no longer able to meet the reasonable needs of its minority citizens and their lot would worsen as the city faced an ever bleaker financial future. Given the overall situation, the majority of citizens welcomed the World Trade Center project. Yes, they said with a keen appraisal of reality, in the long run it would make the rich richer, but it had to be built, maintained and serviced, and that meant jobs—for some of them at least—and jobs meant income. All in all, building the Twin Towers was seen to be an act of confidence, heralding expectation of a brighter future for New York.

The *Queen Mary* en route to a
Hudson River terminal. New York is
no longer a great passenger port:
during the 1950s-1960s the proud
trans-Atlantic liners steamed into
history, victims of inexpensive air
travel, though some cruise-ship
traffic continues.

world tra

WORLD

CHAPTER

2

THE TWIN TOWERS:
DESIGN AND ARCHITECTURE

38 TOP
A SMILING MINORU YAMASAKI IS
CAPTURED ON FILM IN A PERFECT
PERSPECTIVE AT THE FOOT OF THE
STRUCTURES THAT BROUGHT HIM
WORLDWIDE FAME: THE WORLD TRADE
CENTER'S TWIN TOWERS.

39
A DISTINCTIVE PICTURE OF THE TOWERS
GLISTENING IN THE SUN. THESE SOARING
STRUCTURES OF STEEL, ALUMINUM AND
GLASS HAD A TOTEMIC ROLE: THE
PROPYLAEA OF A WORLD CITY.

The Twin Towers no longer exist. For just thirty years they were the distinctive hallmark of the Manhattan skyline, one of the most famous in the world. More than an intrinsic visual reference point for downtown New York, the city's vital center, they were also the nerve center of the world economy. Yet their record-breaking height, structural design and the basic fact of their presence were always subject to criticism. It was never a secret that architectural critics did not fully support the World Trade Center project or the Twin Towers' size and design.

Two days after the September 11 attack on the Twin Towers, Nicolai Ouroussoff (the *Los Angeles Times'* architectural critic) described the construction of the towers as an act of optimism and outlined the unusually strong symbolism of the World Trade Center. At the same time, he referred to their "limited architectural value."

Richard Ingersoll (Professor of Architecture at Syracuse University in Florence, Italy; visiting professor at the Swiss Federal Institute of Technology, Zurich; founding editor of the *Design Book Review*) went further, claiming that the Twin Towers were a sad, dull place to work, and even considered that their vacuous forms were indicative of an imminent disaster. This negative opinion was not shared by ordinary people, who felt that the towers were a symbol not just of a city, but of an entire system; a liability, however, that the towers were saddled with from the day of their design.

In their book "Architettura Contemporanea" (Milan 1976), the authors and architectural historians Manfredo Tafuri and Francesco Dal Co discussed the WTC as a work that was "out of scale," and guilty of traumatically changing the development and functional balance of Manhattan.

A huge increase in the number of commuters was the project's first consequence, so significant that from 1966 on, Governor Nelson Rockefeller pushed for construction of a new city on the water—Battery Park City—with the aim of alleviating travel problems and exploiting the new skyscrapers' location. The initial 1966 plans for Battery Park City were by Wallace Harrison and his collaborators. In fact, according to Tafuri and Dal Co, Battery Park City, Roosevelt Island, and the World Trade Center together represented what Raymond Hood (1881-1934) had envisioned in his futuristic master plan, "Manhattan 1950." Discussion of the WTC project inevitably leads to its Japanese-American architect, Minoru Yamasaki (1912-1986), assisted by Emory Roth, whose reputation was made by the WTC project. Architectural historians and critics prefer some of Yamasaki's other major works over the WTC. These include the St. Louis airport (1935-55), designed with G.F. Hellmuth and J. Leinweber (a terminal typified by a series of slender intersected cylindrical vaults covering the passenger waiting area), the Society of Arts and Crafts building (Detroit, 1958); the American Concrete Institute building (Detroit, 1959), or the Reynolds Metals Offices, also in Detroit (1959). The most typical elements of Yamasaki's work are vaults that mask structural elements of the walls, often formed by profiled modules made from concrete or other agglomerates.

After studying architecture at the universities in Washington and New York, Yamasaki worked for Shreve, Lamb and Harmon—the architects of the Empire State Building—where perhaps the idea was born and nursed that, one day, he could compete with the masters. The masters Yamasaki most admired were Mies van der Rohe and Le Corbusier.

The WTC was conceived in 1962, began to take form in 1964, and the first construction started in 1966. The towers' distinctive features were geometric divisions, glass walls, and load-bearing

columns. The North Tower was completed in 1971, and the South in 1974, when the WTC complex was inaugurated.

Strongly promoted by the Port Authority of New York and New Jersey, the WTC was a sensational project for the period, aimed at bringing into being a commercial district of great visual impact in a depressed area. It occupied (it is sad to have to refer to it in the past tense) a total ground area of over 15 acres, and the Plaza at the base of the towers exceeded five acres in extent.

Yamasaki believed deeply in the project, stating, "The World Trade Center must . . . become the living representation of the faith of man in humanity, of his need for individual dignity, of his trust in co-operation and, through this, of his ability to find greatness."

The WTC's immense scale is reflected in the extraordinary statistics that describe the 10-year project, to use a rather dry term for a mighty undertaking. In addition to the towers (1 and 2 WTC) were five other buildings and an immense subterranean shopping mall. No. 3 WTC was the Marriott Hotel (designed by Skidmore, Owings and Merrill, and built in 1971 as the Vista Hotel); 4 WTC housed the Commodities Exchange; 6 WTC was the 8-story U.S. Customs House. The remainder were office buildings. To a greater or lesser extent, all were destroyed by the collapse of the towers.

The Twin Towers were each roughly 1,360 feet high, 196 feet long on each side, had 110 floors and 104 elevators. They rested on foundations that penetrated 69 feet into the bedrock. Construction required 200,000 tons of steel and 3,000 miles of electrical cable to satisfy the daily distribution and consumption of about 80,000 kilowatts. For express elevator ascent, the structures were divided into three vertical zones. The towers had over 43,000 windows, each one 22 inches wide. In total, the façades required some 215,000 square feet of glass.

The initial stage was the clearance and excavation of 12,000,000 square feet of land, with the preservation

42 TOP AND 43 TOP
YAMASAKI PRODUCED MANY MODELS
BEFORE THE FINAL DESIGN OF THE
TWIN TOWERS WAS AGREED UPON.
POTENTIAL SOLUTIONS HAD CONSIDERED
MORE TOWERS—SMALLER, NATURALLY,
THAN THE FINAL DESIGN—AS A
COMPROMISE TO SATISFY THE PA'S
REQUIREMENT FOR A SPECIFIC AMOUNT
OF USEABLE OFFICE SPACE.

42-43 BOTTOM
MINORU YAMASAKI SEEMS TO WANT TO
DISPEL ALL DOUBT AS HE DISCUSSES THE
WORLD TRADE CENTER'S SURFACE AREA.
THE 15 ACRES THE PA ACQUIRED IN A
DEPRESSED AREA WERE TO BE USED TO
BUILD A COMPLEX DESTINED TO BE, AS
YAMSASAKI STATED, A "LIVING
REPRESENTATION OF THE FAITH OF MAN
IN HUMANITY."

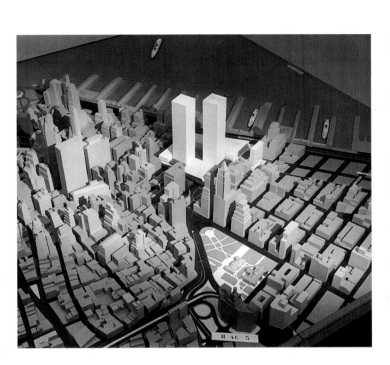

(and re-routing) of the New York-New Jersey subterranean railway lines, and accommodation for the New York subway and pedestrian passageways.

Yamasaki produced about one hundred models before choosing the two towers, which represented a breakthrough configuration compromise. This option offered the possibility of creating the required ten million square feet of office space. In designing the towers, Yamasaki went beyond the existing principles of skyscraper construction (the U.S.'s most important contribution to architecture), making skillful use of technology and materials.

The structural system was simple and effective. The façades (196 ft wide) were to all effects a cage made of steel and prefabricated sections (in modules measuring 10 x 32 feet), able to resist wind-induced and seismic strains without transferring stress to the towers' core structure, but distributing and absorbing it throughout the outer wall structure. The structures were highly resistant yet light, without internal columns beyond the elevator core.

Designed to resist atmospheric agents, seismic events and even accidental intrusion (including being hit by an airliner), the Twin Towers were unable to withstand the heat caused by flaming combustion of the 20,000 gallons of jet fuel spilt into each tower on September 11. The heat literally detached the concrete-clad floors from the towers' steel core and exterior walls. These, having lost their characteristics of resistance and flexibility because of excessive heat, gave way under the weight of the structure.

It is certainly right, though perhaps a little premature, to consider a future for the WTC site and to document the unexpected argument that pits supporters of the creation of a memorial against the faction of "rebuilders." Renzo Piano, who was recently received a commission to design the New York Times' new midtown offices, states that he favors construction of new skyscrapers, though perhaps not so high—only 656 feet.

The proposal by two artists and two architects (Julian La Verdière and Paul Myoda; John Bennet and Gustavo Monteverdi) is more spectacular and verges on kitsch; their idea is the temporary creation of two towers of light, the diaphanous representation of what used to stand on the site.

More simply and realistically, what remains of one of the most famous, debated and daring projects of American—or even world—architecture is the knowledge of its absence, its memory and the warning it provides.

44

A LARGE SCALE MODEL WAS SET OUT FOR A PHOTOGRAPHIC SESSION. BASED ON A HUMAN SCALE, THE SIZE OF THE PRE-EXISTING BUILDINGS AND THE MAJESTY OF THE TOWERS ARE CLEARLY EVIDENT; ONCE ERECTED, THEY WOULD DOMINATE THE SURROUNDING BUILDINGS FROM AN IMMENSE HEIGHT.

45

THE *DEUS EX MACHINA* OF A PROJECT ABOUT TO BE SET IN MOTION, ARCHITECT MINORU YAMASAKI'S THOUGHTS ARE PROBABLY DIVIDED BETWEEN THE KNOWLEDGE OF A SUCCESSFUL DESIGN AND THE CHALLENGE OF EXECUTION, WITH THE INEVITABLE ADJUSTMENTS AND UNEXPECTED PROBLEMS THAT WILL EMERGE DURING CONSTRUCTION. IT TOOK 8 YEARS FROM THE START OF THE EXCAVATION IN 1966 TO THE INAUGURATION IN 1973, BUT THE WORLD TRADE CENTER BEGAN ITS INDEPENDENT WORKING LIFE AS EARLY AS 1971.

Labels within the plan:

U.S. CUSTOMS HOUSE

NORTHEAST PLAZA BUILDING

NORTH TOWER

FIVE ACRES PLAZA

HOTEL UNDER STUDY

SOUTH TOWER

SOUTHEAST PLAZA BUILDING

46 TOP
IN THIS VIEW OF THE MODEL, THE PLAZA
OF THE COMPLEX, THOUGH ENORMOUS,
SEEMS TO HAVE BEEN SACRIFICED AND
TRAMPLED BY THE MASSIVE BULK OF THE
TOWERS.

46 BOTTOM
PERHAPS THE PAVING OF THE PLAZA—
SHOWN HERE IN PLAN—WAS SUPPOSED TO
MITIGATE THE INSISTENTLY ORTHOGONAL
DESIGN OF THE COMPLEX.

47
THE MODEL CLEARLY SHOWS THE TOWERS'
THREE MODULES. THEY WERE CHOSEN
FROM OVER ONE HUNDRED MODELS AS THE
IDEAL MORPHOLOGICAL COMPROMISE.

48-49
Over 66 feet of rock had to be removed to provide sufficient foundations to anchor the towers to the ground. The apocalyptic pit shown here contains the framework necessary for the excavation to be accomplished.

48 bottom
All the power lines, air inlets and telephone cables ran beneath each floor. The buildings were equipped with complex heating and energy management systems that were extremely modern for the era.

49 bottom
Another city lay beneath the World Trade Center: it comprised car parks, subway and railway lines, miles of cables and the massive machinery needed to maintain the vertical metropolis in operation.

Concrete

Telephone and Power Outlets

Floor Tile

Corrugated Steel Truss Covering

Heating, Ventilating and Air Conditioning Duct

Utility Ducts: Telephone and Power

Vesey St.

Greenwich St.

Old PATH tube

Tracks for
new PATH terminal

West St.

Old PATH tube

Liberty St.

Steel tieback tendons
anchored to outlying rock

50 TOP
THIS VIEW SHOWS THE STEEL LOAD-BEARING
STRUCTURE OF THE TOWERS AND THE
ANCHORING OF THE METAL COLUMNS TO THE
PLINTH MADE OF REINFORCED CONCRETE.

50 CENTER
THE STEEL MODULES (EACH MEASURING
10X33 FEET) EMERGE FROM THE BEDROCK TO
SUPPORT THE TWIN TOWERS—THE WORLD'S
TALLEST BUILDINGS AT THE TIME OF THE
PROJECT'S INAUGURATION.

50 BOTTOM
THESE DRAWINGS SHOW THE PHASES OF
EXCAVATION, INSERTION OF THE REINFORCING
FRAMEWORK, AND THE FINAL CASTING OF
THE FOUNDATIONS OF THE PERIMETER WALLS.

51
THIS PHOTO GIVES A GOOD INDICATION OF
THE DEPTH OF THE FOUNDATIONS. ON THE
RIGHT ARE THE PERIMETER WALLS; ON THE
LEFT THE STEEL FRAMEWORK IS BEING BUILT.

52
THE CONSTRUCTION SYSTEM FOR THE TWIN TOWERS IS CLEARLY SHOWN HERE: A SUPPORT CORE, THE ELEVATOR SHAFTS AND PLANTS, AND THE STRONG "SELF-SUPPORTING" PERIMETER FRAMEWORK.

53 TOP
THE BARE STRUCTURE OF THE STEEL FRAMEWORK HAS NOT YET BEEN COVERED WITH THE UNINTERRUPTED ROWS OF SMALL WINDOWS (ONLY 22 INCHES WIDE); THEY WILL GIVE AN IMPRESSION OF HARMONIZED STRENGTH AND FLEXIBILITY.

53 CENTER
THIS DRAWING CLEARLY SHOWS HOW THE PREFABRICATED SECTIONS OF THE FLOORS RESTED ON BOTH THE CENTRAL CORE AND THE STRONG PERIMETER SECTIONS.

53 BOTTOM
A MOMENT DURING THE ANCHORING OF THE STEEL MODULES BY SKILLED STEEL ERECTORS ACCUSTOMED TO WORKING ON HIGH-RISE TOWERS.

2

54-55
A STRIKING PHOTOGRAPH OF LOWER
MANHATTAN WITH THE NOT YET
COMPLETED TOWERS ALREADY DECLARING
THEIR IMPOSING PRESENCE. THEIR ACRES
OF WINDOWS WOULD HAVE BEEN
SUFFICIENT FOR THE NEEDS OF A TOWN OF
10,000 INHABITANTS.

110th fl.   5

Zone
Three

78th fl.   4
                                                  5

Zone
Two

44th fl.   4
                                                  5

Zone
One

                                                  5

Con-
course
           1 2   3 3 3 3   2

55 TOP
THE VERTICAL THRUST OF THE FAÇADE
CLEARLY SHOWS THE HORIZONTAL SECTION
BREAKS AT 1/3RD AND AGAIN AT 2/3RDS OF
HEIGHT. YAMASAKI'S DESIGN CALLED FOR
THE TOWERS TO BE MADE UP OF THREE
ALMOST IDENTICAL SECTIONS.

55 BOTTOM
THE THREE-SECTION STRUCTURE WAS ALSO
REFLECTED IN THE ARRANGEMENT OF THE
SUPERFAST ELEVATORS (104 IN EACH
TOWER).

DESIGN AND ARCHITECTURE

55

59
In this photo taken at the beginning of the 1980s, the Twin Towers are reflected in the waters of the Hudson: no other structures have yet been built between them and the riverfront.

60-63
Impressive by day, the towers were more so at night, when, in the warm light of sunset, they rose like cyclopic twin lighthouses in the darkness of New York.

56
In this bird's eye view of the World Trade Center the towers dominate the Plaza and the other buildings of the complex.

57 top
The Plaza at the exact moment the shadow of the South Tower is thrown onto the corner of the North Tower to create a fascinating play of light.

57 center and bottom
The World Trade Center is complete: the year is 1973 (as the clothes worn to the inauguration ceremony suggest). Note that the landfill in the Hudson River, on which the World Financial Center will be built, is still empty.

Legend:

- Collapsed buildings
- Partly collapsed buildings
- Buildings with major damage
- Buildings with structural damage
- Buildings damaged but stable, ready for occupancy with repairs/cleaning
- Buildings which need cleaning
- Buildings not affected

100 GOLD

MAP OF DISASTER AREA

COLLAPSED BUILDINGS:
1 - 1 World Trade Center
2 - 2 World Trade Center
3 - 7 World Trade Center
4 - 5 World Trade Center
5 - North Bridge

PARTLY COLLAPSED BUILDINGS:
6 - 6 World Trade Center
7 - Marriott Hotel
8 - 4 World Trade Center
9 - One Liberty Plaza

BUILDINGS WITH MAJOR DAMAGE:
10 - East River Savings Bank
11 - Federal Building
12 - 3 World Financial Center
13 - St. Nicholas Church
14 - 90 West Street
15 - Bankers Trust
16 - South Bridge

BUILDINGS WITH STRUCTURAL DAMAGE:
17 - Millennium Hilton
18 - 2 World Financial Center
19 - 1 World Financial Center
20 - 30 West Broadway
21 - Winter Garden
22 - N.Y. Telephone Building
23 - 4 World Financial Center

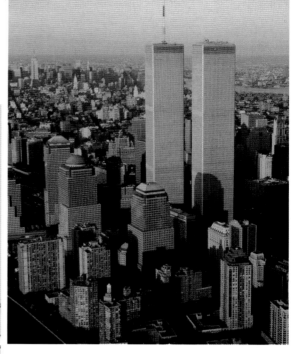

64-65 AND 65 BOTTOM
THE AXONOMETRIC VIEW SHOWN HERE
(WITH THE PLAN TO THE RIGHT) SHOWS
THE SITUATION BEFORE AND AFTER THE
ATTACK ON SEPTEMBER 11. A SURPRISING
NUMBER OF NEARBY BUILDINGS SUFFERED
SEVERE STRUCTURAL DAMAGE.

65 TOP RIGHT
THE NEW WORLD FINANCIAL CENTER IS
COMPLETE. DESIGNED BY CÉSAR PELLI
(1981-1987), THE TOWERS ROSE ON
LANDFILL IN THE HUDSON RIVER, JUST
WEST OF THE WORLD TRADE CENTER AND
ADJOINING BATTERY PARK CITY.

66 -67
LOWER MANHATTAN AS IT APPEARED FROM
OVERHEAD JUST BEFORE AND AFTER THE
TERRIBLE ATTACK ON SEPTEMBER 11.

A CATALYST FOR
CREATIVITY

The Twin Towers became instant icons. Almost all architectural critics and propounders of the higher aesthetic condemned or dismissed them, often as casually as the public dismisses critics. The towers were too brash, too big, and too dominant, shattering the urban scale, overburdening the area. But New Yorkers on the whole admired the Twin Towers as quintessential examples of the city's "can do" energy and reflections of their own enthusiasm for the best and the newest—even if it had to be the biggest. An additional factor played a role in humanizing the Twin Towers. Three events occurring within five years, each unique in New York's history, endowed the Twin Towers with a special mystique, a magnetism that made New Yorkers realize the towers challenged the human imagination. The towers themselves had entered the record book with a plethora of 'firsts.' Now, by simply existing, they caused new 'firsts' to happen and enter the record.

The first event occurred on August 7, 1974, when New Yorkers left home for work to the surprising news that Philippe Petit, a 24-year-old French citizen, had successfully secured a tightrope between the towers and had made several elegant and seemingly carefree crossings. Contemporary reports made it clear that the PA, New York police and the public had experienced much anxiety—and that Philippe Petit had not.

The second event occurred a little over a year later, on July 22, 1975. That morning Owen Quinn, a 24-year-old New Yorker, made a parachute jump from the roof of the North Tower. Though quickly executed and not unduly complicated, Quinn's jump was dramatic and not without danger. After his safe but bruising landing, the Port Authority charged him with criminal trespass, concerned to discourage other risk-takers. The move did not succeed. On May 26, 1977, another New Yorker, George Willig, aged 27, achieved an exciting first. Using clamps that he had designed to lock into grooves in the tower's façade, he made a three-hour ascent from base to rooftop, a time-span that greatly pleased the media and enthralled a worldwide audience.

Almost effortlessly the Twin Towers promoted themselves. The five-acre Plaza from which they rose was a pedestrian haven removed from vehicular traffic, its focal point a vast fountain and massive bronze spherical sculpture whose sweeping curve was in dramatic contrast to the unbroken vertical lines of the towers. A full calendar of planned and impromptu events—music, theater and other—made the Plaza a place of endlessly changing scenes. The Plaza, bigger than the Piazza of San Marco in Venice, was a natural starting point for pleasurable activity. Beyond it was the bridge to the World Financial Center and the Winter Garden, opening onto the Marina and

the Battery Park City Esplanade and the Hudson River. To the south rose the familiar New York Harbor icon, the Statue of Liberty. Below the Plaza was the Concourse, a permanent magnet for the compulsive shopper.

Two predictable but rewarding features drew visitors and New Yorkers alike to the Twin Towers. The enclosed observation deck on the 107th floor of the South Tower, with its access to the roof, opened in December 1975 and became an instant hit. The deck did not overtake the Empire State Building's 86th-floor open-air observation terrace; fortunately, each offered the best vista in at least one direction. The World Trade Center's observation deck offered stunning views to the south, over New York Harbor and Brooklyn. From the Empire State Building's deck, Central Park unrolling to the north seems only a stone's throw away. Both attractions drew over 1.5 million paying viewers per year; neither complained of being edged out of the market.

In the North Tower, the fashionable *Windows on the World* restaurant on the 107th floor opened in April 1976, and quickly became renowned for an imaginative menu and an excellent wine list. For hundreds of thousands of New Yorkers and visitors, *Windows on the World* offered lunch with unrivalled panoramic views. Drinks and dinner à deux there, above the city's myriad lights, with the Staten

72 AND 73
"THE SPHERE," A 27-FOOT-HIGH BRONZE
SCULPTURE, WAS THE FOCAL POINT OF THE
TWIN TOWERS' 5-ACRE PLAZA. THE
GERMAN SCULPTOR FRITZ KOENIG
DESIGNED THE MUCH-ADMIRED WORK.

Island ferries crossing the black waters below like programmed fireflies, was the launching-pad for countless memorable romances.

On the movie front the Twin Towers quickly reached the screen. The 1976 remake of "King Kong" (first filmed in 1933), had as its unforgettable climax a hunted King Kong leaping from tower to tower, a terrified Jessica Lange clutched in his mighty paw, moments before his fatal plunge. For once, the Empire State Building was dramatically upstaged. Because New York and Lower Manhattan are perennially popular locations for shooting movies, the Twin Towers appeared on screen time and time again, if only in fleeting exterior shots. Practical considerations, security issues and cost made it very difficult to set up and shoot within the towers, though they feature prominently in mock-up or reality in a number of films. Among the better known are Woody Allen's nostalgic "Manhattan" (1979, Diane Keaton, Meryl Streep); "Escape from New York" (1981, Kurt Russell), featuring the towers in a futuristic horror movie; "Wall Street" (1987, Michael Douglas and Charlie Sheen); and "Working Girl" (1988, Sigourney Weaver and Harrison Ford), in which the ambitious Melanie Griffith gazes up at the Twin Towers, a symbol of unbounded ambition, a salute to success. "Godzilla" (1998, Mathew Broderick and Maria Pitilli) was a return to the fantastic.

By 1980 the Twin Towers image was undeniably entrenched in the public mind, and its use has never lessened. Channel 11, a major New York TV station, adapted the Twin Towers' profile and adopted the design as a logo, placing it on countless TV screens day in and day out. Liquor companies, including Maker's Mark Bourbon and Bacardi Rum, have used the image in high-profile advertising campaigns; numerous other companies have featured the Twin Towers on merchandise or on shopping bags or promotions. Fine photography has captured the Twin Towers from endless angles; vertical candles in the dusk cut by the curving light-laced horizontal of Brooklyn Bridge, or rising across the Harbor, above and beyond Lady Liberty's familiar high-held torch, or in closer shots, framing the classic façade of St. Paul's Chapel.

Approaching Lower Manhattan from New Jersey, from Staten Island, from Brooklyn or Long Island, the Twin Towers dominate the skyline. They are never just there; they are powerfully, strikingly there. Seen from the Brooklyn Heights Esplanade, the Twin Towers become almost magical. They shimmer in the brilliant morning light of a spring day; at dusk in winter they are pillars of light in a darkened sky.

And now the Twin Towers and so much else around them are gone; utterly destroyed in a psychopathic act of mindless hatred. Without doubt, new buildings will rise. Some suggest a memorial within a park; others ask for housing; still others suggest a defiant rebuilding of the WTC and Twin Towers complex. The economic, demographic, employment, and transportation calculus is vastly changed from that of the 1970s; whatever is built must be governed by sensitive interpretation of new criteria.

It is too soon to invest in plans and schedules: the current chapter is not yet closed; the tragedy is too recent and too raw. But what the WTC stood for cannot, must not, be forgotten. Minoru Yamasaki, the quiet, thoughtful architect of the World Trade Center, captured that purpose in words that will not be surpassed:

"World trade means world peace and consequently the World Trade Center buildings in New York. . . had a bigger purpose than just to provide room for tenants. The World Trade Center is a living symbol of man's dedication to world peace. . . beyond the compelling need to make this a monument to world peace, the World Trade Center should, because of its importance, become a representation of man's belief in humanity, his need for individual dignity, his belief in the cooperation of men, and through cooperation, his ability to find greatness."

74 TOP
ON A CLEAR DAY, THE SOUTH TOWER
ROOFTOP VIEW EXTENDED ALMOST 50
MILES IN ALL DIRECTIONS. THE STUNNING
PANORAMA OF NEW YORK HARBOR
REMINDED VIEWERS THAT THE CITY WAS
FOUNDED AS A PORT.

74-75
A PURIST MIGHT DEEM THE WORLD
FINANCIAL CENTER AND THE WORLD
TRADE CENTER TO BE STRICTLY "BUSINESS
BUILDINGS," BUT THE GENERAL PUBLIC
FOUND FASCINATING COMBINATIONS OF
FORM, TEXTURE, AND CONFIGURATION.

75 BOTTOM
THE WINTER GARDEN BROUGHT
WHIMSICAL ELEGANCE TO THE ADJOINING
WORLD FINANCIAL AND WORLD TRADE
CENTERS' BUSINESS ENVIRONMENT. A FULL
CULTURAL EVENTS CALENDAR MADE THE
GARDEN A POPULAR FORUM FOR NEW
YORKERS AND VISITORS ALIKE.

76
HELEN FRANKENTHALER, A NEW YORK
PAINTER GREATLY ADMIRED AS AN ABSTRACT
EXPRESSIONIST, EXECUTED THIS STRIKING MAJOR
WORK, MOUNTED IN THE TOWER LOBBY.

77
ONE QUARTER OF A TWIN TOWER WRAP-
AROUND LOBBY, WITH THE ELEVATOR CORE
AT LEFT. OPENNESS AND SPACIOUSNESS
WERE KEY DESIGN ELEMENTS THROUGHOUT
THE WTC; HENCE THE 10-STORY LOBBY.

78 BOTTOM
"MEET YOU IN THE WINDOWS ON THE
WORLD!" A GREAT NEW YORK
EXPERIENCE: DESIGN, DÉCOR, FOOD, WINE,
MOOD AND MOMENT CAME TRIUMPHANTLY
TOGETHER. IF WORDS FAILED, THERE WAS
ALWAYS THE VIEW . . .

78-79
THE WINTER GARDEN ADDED WHIMSICAL
ELEGANCE TO THE TRADE AND FINANCIAL
CENTERS, AND DRAMATIC LIGHTING ADDED
TO ITS MANY SPECIAL EVENTS. THE PALM
TREES HAVE SEEN IT ALL . . .

80
FILMING "KING KONG"
(JOHN GUILLERMAN, 1976) CALLED
FOR CROWD SCENES, PARTICULARLY
IN DYING KONG'S FALL TO THE PLAZA.
NEW YORKERS JUST LOVED BEING PART
OF THE ACTION . . .

81
IN "INDEPENDENCE DAY," ALIENS FROM
OUTER SPACE CAST A GIANT SHADOW,
THREATENING THE TWIN TOWERS,
NEW YORK AND THE NATION.

THE NEW HEART OF
THE FINANCIAL DISTRICT

84
THE TWIN TOWERS, SOARING ABOVE THE
WORLD FINANCIAL CENTER, TAKE ON A
GOLDEN GLOW REFLECTING THE LATE
AFTERNOON SUN.

85
TWO NEW YORK ICONS SALUTE ONE
ANOTHER: LADY LIBERTY AND THE TWIN
TOWERS.

Over its thirty-year life span, the World Trade Center—the Twin Towers and the five smaller buildings, including the Marriott Hotel—was a driving force in the revitalization of Lower Manhattan and the Financial District. For hundreds of millions throughout the world, the Twin Towers symbolized the power of American capitalism. But that was not the primary goal, and it's important to remember who financed and built the WTC, what its original purpose was, and how through natural synergies that purpose expanded and changed.

Ironically enough, the brilliant, bold, and hugely successful idea for the WTC came from a powerful but low-profile government agency that financed itself from airport and marine terminal user fees and from bridge and tunnel tolls, accruing large surpluses that it needed to invest. The agency was the Port Authority of New York and New Jersey (the PA), founded in 1921 to "improve trade and commerce." At first, the PA's main activity was operating marine cargo ports on the New York-New Jersey waterfronts. In the 1930s the PA built the George Washington Bridge across the Hudson, linking New York and New Jersey. It also operated the existing airports, and after World War II built new and vastly bigger ones. By the late 1950s, maritime trade

became more competitive and less expansionary. New York felt the squeeze; almost all the docks were to close down by the 1960s, the victim of crowded access streets, expensive warehousing and trucking, and high labor costs. On the New Jersey side, the dock environment was more favorable and the PA was more aggressive, building Port Elizabeth and Port Newark in the late 1940s-early 1950s as new, high efficiency, fast turnaround docks for huge container ships and tankers.

At the beginning of the 1960s, the PA had money and needed public-benefit projects on which to spend it. A trade center was one possibility, soon backed by the financial sector (the loosely allied banks, real estate tycoons, and major investors), which realized that a major new office complex would revitalize Lower Manhattan, an area within minutes of Wall Street. If the PA's financial resources met most or all of the costs, so much the better. If, in keeping with its charter to "improve commerce and trade," the PA brought in numerous businesses involved in these activities, so much the better; the situation between them and the Wall Street money men would be collaborative rather than competitive.

In the late 1960s the New York-New Jersey region was declining as a trade and shipping center, with Houston and New Orleans

growing rapidly. New York needed a dramatic, high profile project to help it and the region recapture pre-eminence in trade and associated finance. Whole areas of the city were deteriorating; Lower Manhattan urgently needed revitalization, urban renewal had passed it by and decay was evident. The Hudson waterfront area to the northwest of Wall Street, was ripe for redevelopment, particularly some thirty blocks of old, low-rise small and mid-sized business buildings. A brand new World Trade Center for the export, import, shipping, insurance and financing communities could be a powerful catalyst for growth. In short, the World Trade Center was an idea whose time had come, and as such it drew powerful political and financial support.

Big projects meant big money, and everybody wanted a piece of the action. Hundreds of issues had to be resolved, including the size, scope, and governance of the project and its financing, land acquisition, design, transportation, and taxation. The states of New York and New Jersey and New York City had vested but differing interests and requirements. Wall Street, the banks, and the great financiers had differing and often competing interests.

Knowing that some industries and businesses would benefit and others might be hurt (including major real estate and office-

86 BOTTOM
THE VIEW ALONG THE WEST SIDE HIGHWAY
TOWARD THE WORLD FINANCIAL CENTER
CONFIRMS MANHATTAN'S TOTAL LOSS OF
PASSENGER AND FREIGHT SHIPPING.

86-87
THE WINTER GARDEN'S CURVILINEAR
STEEL-AND-GLASS CONSTRUCTION IS IN
DRAMATIC CONTRAST TO THE NORTH
TOWER'S VERTICAL MODULARITY.

leasing companies), powerful real estate, business and financial groups tried to shape the project. Among the voices of protest were small business owners, shopkeepers and residents who would be ousted. They were surprisingly effective in getting heard and winning sympathy, but the PA was a governmental entity with power of eminent domain—able to "buy" land from owners unwilling to sell. Thus owners and businesses were sacrificed to the juggernaut of "progress." Despite powerful criticism about the PA's entry into the commercial and real estate market places, New York and New Jersey, with an eye to economic benefits, passed the legislation that enabled the PA to proceed. They recognized that older office buildings were losing tenants to newer ones; some major financial and brokerage houses had moved to newer, more efficient and utilitarian buildings in Mid-Manhattan. The WTC would be the dynamo of the economic revival and urban renewal of Lower Manhattan, so the Twin Towers became a reality.

The World Trade Center never became what its name advertised and over time anticipation and actuality moved ever farther apart. For a decade or so the WTC courted maritime, trade, and related businesses, without ever becoming the single hub for them. New York State and the PA rented very substantial amounts of space; neither were remotely trade organizations. In the 1980s, WTC rents began to move from below-market to equal to or above-market rates. Smaller tenants left the WTC; banks, brokerage houses, insurance companies and law firms moved in, reflecting a wide-ranging mix with fewer trade companies.

With the Twin Towers unrivalled as the defining feature of the Manhattan skyline, and the busy, vibrant five-acre Plaza between the towers well established as a popular meeting place, the WTC began to replace Wall Street as the biggest tourist magnet in Lower Manhattan. Differentiations of roles and activities further blurred during the 1980s and 1990s. The establishment of the Commodities Exchange at 4 WTC and construction of the privately funded World Financial Center, immediately west of the WTC, further expanded the old Financial

District, traditionally centered on Wall Street and concentrated to the southeast. Increasingly, for younger New Yorkers and for tourists of all ages, the WTC typified the Financial District and was its visible, beating heart. Summer and winter alike visitors and tourists streamed across the covered bridge connecting the WTC to the World Financial Center. It was leisurely stroll down through the elegant crystal palace of the Winter Garden, out onto the Hudson River waterfront and to the parks and handsome esplanade that add amenity and elegance to the new apartment blocks of Battery Park City.

The standard circuit took visitors back across a second covered bridge and south to the narrow streets that lead over to Wall Street. Then it's back to the WTC and the vast shopping and dining Concourse below. There a huge range of stores, many of them decidedly fashionable, catered to every consumer whim. The air-conditioned Concourse became a place to visit in its own right; busy, exciting and offering every sort of culinary treat—a very comforting escapist world.

No resident or worker or visitor in the Financial District could for even a moment forget the soaring presence of the silvery, clean-lined Twin Towers. They and the adjoining buildings housed a vibrant community of more than 50,000 people from all over the world; the best, the brightest, and the most confident. In a thousand ways a day they made opportunity, created markets and business, and moved money and goods. Their presence and energy fueled a small world of restaurants and stores, bazaars and boutiques, cafes and conversations. Enthusiasm for life was palpable; walking across the Plaza in the sunny high noon of a perfect New York day or in a brilliantly lit early evening, the message in the air was: "Dream it; do it." It was a very fitting message. The World Trade Center began as an almost impossible dream: it became, if only briefly, a dream realized, a whole new world.

90
MANIPULATING ARCHITECTURAL REALITY BY
CONVERTING THE WTC'S VERTICAL LINES
INTO THE CURVES AND DIAGONALS OF
EVER-CHANGING CONFIGURATIONS IS A
FASCINATING PHOTOGRAPHIC CHALLENGE.

91
TWO SYMBOLS JUXTAPOSED: THE ICONS
OF THE NATION AND ITS ECONOMIC POWER
STRAIN FOR THE SKY; AT THEIR BASE
STANDS ALEXANDER CALDER'S RED
METALLIC SCULPTURE.

92 AND 93
THE GENEROUSLY SPACED YET SLENDER
VERTICALS IN THE TWIN TOWER LOBBIES
AND THE CONTRASTINGLY MUSCULAR
HORIZONTAL BANDS COMBINE TO SUGGEST
STRENGTH AND OPENNESS—A NECESSARY
ELEMENT CONSIDERING THE VAST HUMAN
FLOWS PASSING THROUGH THE LOBBIES AT
9:00 A.M. AND 5:00 P.M.

FROM PAGE 94 TO PAGE 99
IN AUTUMN THE NEW YORK SKY IS ALWAYS
CHANGING, SOMETIMES BLUE, SOMETIMES
CLOUDY. THE OUTLINE OF THE CITY AND ITS
DETAILS CHANGE WITH THE LIGHT: IT IS

FAIRY-LIKE WHEN VEILED BY THE MORNING
MIST OR ATTENUATED BY THE SOFT COLORS
OF DAWN, AND IT APPEARS STRONG AND
MAJESTIC WHEN SCULPTED BY THE LAST
RAYS OF THE EVENING SUN.

100-101
EMPHASIZED BY THE NIGHT LIGHTS, THE
TWIN TOWERS RISE BEHIND BROOKLYN
BRIDGE. THE BRIDGE WAS DESIGNED BY
THE GERMAN ARCHITECT, JOHN AUGUSTUS
ROEBLING AND OPENED IN 1883.

SEPTEMBER 11, 2001

The flamebursts and plumes of smoke are seared into people's memories worldwide. No event in the history became known throughout the world so quickly or so dramatically, or was so symbolic. The Twin Towers rise 1,360 feet in the center of one of the world's most densely populated cities. It's likely that more people saw the flames, the smoke, and the collapse of the shimmering Twin Towers with their own eyes than ever witnessed any other urban disaster.

Within the hour on that warm, sunny morning there was nothing that anyone could say that was new or different: TV commentators left no thought unexpressed. People spoke to comfort each other or to break through the numbness that shock produced rather than to make any informative statement. The suddenness, the enormity and the totality of the event was overwhelming; it is impossible to comprehend such virulent hate, such murderous intent.

The multiple-thrust response to the attack showed near-miraculous efficiency and focus. The speed of action, the scale of operations, and the courage of all who participated make for a memorable chapter in the nation's history.

Heroism was the characteristic of the day. A woman in a wheel chair is carried down endless flights of stairs, a blind man and his dog are escorted down, people assist the injured and disabled. Executives making a last check that all employees are safely out leave too late to save themselves. Some

twenty senior World Trade Center staff perish on site, ensuring others will survive. The Fire Department's chaplain, giving the Last Rites to dying firemen, becomes a victim. The courage that kept firemen, police officers, and other rescue personnel in the danger zone, helping people to escape, cost them their lives when the towers collapsed.

New York's Emergency Command Center—in the WTC—was totally destroyed; nonetheless, emergency plans clicked in instantly. Within minutes, disciplined teams of rescue personnel were doing everything the flame-wracked, smoke-billowing site allowed for. Fire engines and ambulances raced down traffic-free avenues; hospitals in Manhattan and neighboring New Jersey moved into emergency operating mode—for all too few survivors.

In Greenwich Village, a mile and a half north of the WTC, people flooded onto the streets within minutes of the first attack. Most witnessed the collapse of the South Tower at 9:50 a.m., while the North Tower, still billowing flame and smoke, collapsed at 10:29. Horrified watchers saw people jumping from high floors, tiny colored dots within the flumes of falling débris. A sense of the unreal—the surreal—pervaded; people looked into the eyes of complete strangers, uncomprehending. Many clasped each other; some sat on the curbs; some sobbed, knowing that people they loved were dying or must have died in horrific circumstances. The Village cafés had their TV sets

locked to the news channel; people watch blankly, unable to speak.

Everything known was instantly broadcast, but little new information was forthcoming. No one would (or perhaps could) estimate the death toll. It was a morning of endless streams of people shambling north up the Avenue of the Americas. Most were in shock, many layered in ash and soot, holding onto companions while local residents desperately dialed on cell-phones, trying to put victims in touch with their families. Here and there exhausted people sat on the sidewalks. Farther south, nearer to Ground Zero, it was worse, with people crowding into building lobbies, bleeding, hysterical or traumatized into silence. In the Village cafés, waitresses gently handed out coffee to those who stumbled in, most dazed though unscratched; the visibly injured or disabled had been picked up farther south. All day long the sirens wailed as emergency vehicles sped south; all day long ambulances raced up the Avenue of the Americas toward St. Vincent's Medical Center. There people were parked all along the hospital forecourt in wheel-chairs— mainly in shock. A huge command post sprang up with well over fifty emergency workers and a hundred volunteers.

The city rapidly went into high alert status, with bridges and tunnels closed and subway and train service suspended. Despite the horrific shock and massive dislocation the attack caused, the call was for the maintenance of order: stay calm, cope with

110
THE EMPIRE STATE BUILDING, SOME 50
BLOCKS NORTH OF THE DEVASTATED
WORLD TRADE CENTER AREA, REMAINS A
FAMILIAR AND COMFORTING PRESENCE.

FROM PAGE 111 TO PAGE 115
AT 9:03, THE SECOND BOEING 767 HIT
THE SOUTH TOWER; THE 767'S 20,000
GALLONS OF JET FUEL IGNITED, CREATING A
BLAZING INFERNO.

FROM PAGE 116 TO PAGE 119
THE SOUTH TOWER, THE SECOND TO BE
HIT, WAS THE FIRST TO COLLAPSE (9:50
A.M.), CONDEMNING THOUSANDS TRAPPED
WITHIN TO A HORRIFIC DEATH.

transportation problems, Move on . . . New York is functioning—shaken but NOT destroyed! The broad artery of Fourteenth Street, running east-west clean across Manhattan, became a manned boundary. To the north, as much normality as possible; to the south, the avenues and streets open to pedestrians only. Further south, Houston (or "First") Street, another major east-west artery, marked a tightly controlled no-access zone; below it, emergency crews and supplies were assembling.

By 6:00 p.m. the patient inflow to the hospitals had diminished to a trickle; no more survivors could be found. The whole WTC area was one vast mound of smoking rubble, hundreds of feet high, spilling over into adjacent streets. The news coverage was of course constant—terrible figures flowing out; 78 police officers unaccounted for, 200 firemen unaccounted for. Some 50,000 people work at the WTC; some 20,000 more are in the area on business visits. Those killed would be numbered in the thousands.

By mid-evening limited subway service was operating and outbound bridge and tunnel crossings were restored in an effort to clear Manhattan of non-residents and non-essential outsiders. New Yorkers recognized that effective management was in place and emergency

operations were going according to plan. The street crowds thinned around 8.30 p.m. as people went home to listen to President Bush address the nation. A judicious speech with only the hint of possible military retaliation. But how does a nation retaliate against an enemy whose weapons are furtiveness and stealth, the murder of the innocent, an enemy too cowardly to ever take the field or stand in the light of day? After the president's address, people again took to the streets, restlessly wandering from St. Vincent's down to the Houston Street barriers and back.

Toward midnight a major quasi-military operation became apparent. Convoys of dump-trucks, bulldozers, plank-and-scaffold trucks parked along Houston Street. At intervals they would roll on down the Avenue of the Americas toward the still burning WTC area. The local fire-station became a command post; for a brief time earlier in the day, before more suitable space could be found closer to the WTC, it had been Mayor Giuliani's Command HQ. The local baseball court became a supply depot; nearby the Salvation Army set up mobile canteens.

To the north, St. Vincent's Medical Center was fully established as a major receiving station, the avenue lit up with floodlights and awash with local residents, the media, and would-be

volunteers. These were in excess of need; by noon it had become was clear that there would be few survivors, only a massive hetacomb of entombed dead. Emergency morgues were being set up locally and across the river in New Jersey. Thousands who had not escaped would be burned, or crushed or mangled beyond recognition—with the terrible result that many families would have no closure, no solace of burying their lost. A gruesome task lay ahead: removing the fragmentary remains of what might at first estimates amount to 10,000 bodies.

A month later New Yorkers were going about their business and living their lives. Everywhere, except at Ground Zero and the immediate area, there is at first glance the appearance of normality. It's the second glance that notes the uniformed security guard, the screening device, the cautionary notice. It's those who have taken an airline flight or had business in a government building that know life is not the same. The news is no longer about other countries and other people. At the core, it is about the United States and the challenge it faces. Violence is a threat; vulnerability is a fact of life. The hope must be that justice and sanity prevail. *(Events as viewed from Greenwich Village, NYC).*

FROM PAGE 134 TO PAGE 137
NEW YORK FIRE DEPARTMENT HAS
WRITTEN A TRAGIC AND UNFORGETTABLE
CHAPTER IN THE CITY'S HISTORY.
THE LOSSES: NEW YORK FIRE
DEPARTMENT AND EMERGENCY MEDICAL
SERVICES, 343; PORT AUTHORITY
(WTC MANAGEMENT), 74; NEW YORK
POLICE DEPARTMENT, 23 LIVES.

138 AND 139
ALMOST EVERY NYFD MEMBER LOST
TRUSTED FIREFIGHTER COLLEAGUES; SOME
UNITS HAD ONLY A HANDFUL OF
SURVIVORS. BOTTOM: THE FIRE
DEPARTMENT'S CHAPLAIN, FATHER MYCHAL
JUDGE, WAS AMONG THE HEROES
WHO LOST THEIR LIVES IN THE LINE
OF DUTY.

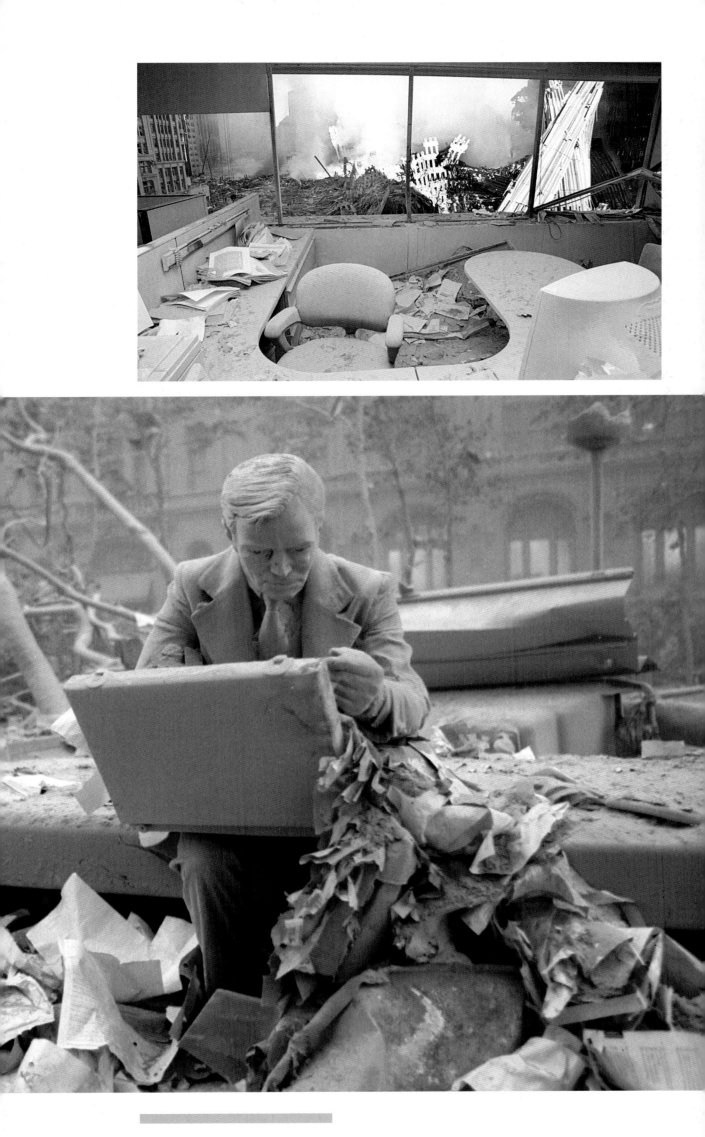

140 TOP AND 141 TOP
SEVERE EXTERNAL AND INTERNAL DAMAGE
AT THE WORLD FINANCIAL CENTER,
ADJOINING THE WORLD TRADE CENTER.

140-141
BURNED DOCUMENTS SYMBOLIZE THE
DISASTER. THE BRONZE "MAN WITH
BRIEFCASE" SYMBOLIZES SURVIVAL AND
FAITH IN THE FUTURE.

142
DANGER, DUST, EXHAUSTION—WITH NO
END IN SIGHT.

143
FOR AMERICANS AND THE WORLD, THE
STARS AND STRIPES ACQUIRED A TRAGIC
NEW ROLE.

144
HALF-BURIED IN RUBBLE, THE WINTER
GARDEN REMAINS INTACT BETWEEN THE
WORLD FINANCIAL CENTER'S TOWERS.

145
THIS AERIAL VIEW, PHOTOGRAPHED
ON SEPTEMBER 26, 2001, SHOWS
THE IMMENSE CRATER RESULTING
FROM THE ATTACK.

146-147
AT NIGHT, THE CLEAN-UP CREWS'
FLOODLIGHTS CAPTURE THE DRAMATIC
SCENE: THE STEEL LATTICE REMNANTS
OF THE TOWERS SUGGEST THE
PORTALS OF HELL.

148-149
THOUSANDS SEEK THEIR LOST ONES—A
TRAGIC QUEST THAT FOR HUNDREDS WILL
HAVE NO FINALITY.

Page 1 of 1

Arnold Lim

FIDUCIARY TRUST COMPANY INTERNATIONAL
(World Trade Center - South Tower)
Title: Programmer / Anaylst
Desk located on 97th floor

Last Contact: Sept. 11, 2001 at 8:50am (5 minutes after the first plane crash)
Race: Asian (Filipino)
Gender: Male
Height: 5'3"
Weight: 180 lbs
Eyes: Brown
Hair: Short Black
Missing From: WTC - South Tower

Notes... ...Silver ball chain necklace, yellow faced silver rolodex, dark brown tanning (indian) skin, black heart leather shoes. Carries an orange/grey Northface backpack, nokia cell phone and possibly a palm pilot.

Contact: Salina Chan (917) 902-8633 or salina_chan19@hotmail.com

WNBC Bulletin Board : WNBC Missing Person Photos : Missing Person Database

9/14/01

THE CHALLENGE
OF THE FUTURE

152
A school child's small, moving tribute, one of many thousands that touched the hearts of New Yorkers.

153
January 2002: clearing the "bathtub." The remains of victims continued to be found as work went on.

The world shared the grief of the bereaved. In London, Queen Elizabeth II attended the service of mourning in St. Paul's Cathedral; in many European cities, crowds gathered silently in the great squares, carrying candles and American flags. Public figures and private citizens brought flowers, proclamations, and messages of condolence to American embassies and consulates worldwide. In mourning, Americans were moved to act: hundreds of communities donated supplies from food to fire-trucks, thousands of specialists volunteered services and skills, millions of citizens gave to financial relief funds. The nation and the world have affirmed that evil cannot conquer.

New York City's fire and police departments, Port Authority personnel, and WTC-area employees continued to serve, experiencing unquantifiable degrees of emotional stress. The arbitrariness of fate; the lack of closure; the helplessness that fire, darkness and shattered communications had imposed; the debt owed to colleagues who had lost their lives; the challenge of the future—all posed burdens. Though assistive services were readily available, recognition of need troubled many of the previously self-sufficient.

Throughout the world, television brought 9/11 directly into children's consciousness. In response, thousands of school children, living in nations at peace or war-torn, created pictures, poems and prayers. Many were exhibited in New York; their power and poignancy struck every viewer; in many they rekindled the innocence of hope. These children's artworks constitute an archive in the making. No school in the WTC area sustained direct major damage on 9/11, though students safely evacuated from the two closest witnessed the horror and chaos of the attack. It is premature to speak definitively of long-term psychological damage to children and parents, but that risk has received a full measure of recognition and response.

As a nation, America has taken strength from the willing support of numerous allies, including those among newer national states. Political leaders have visited Washington, D.C. to confirm support or have spoken unequivocally in national legislatures. It is clear that the imperatives of the campaign against terrorism override political differences among states and can bring together nations of different faiths.

The total cost of 9/11 cannot be easily calculated. Replacement costs for physical structures are roughly calculable but business and tax losses, lost jobs, reduced tourism, increased security costs, and the tragic loss of skilled business leaders and employees are not easily calculated. Add to this the previous business slowdown and a nascent recovery, economic activity to be generated by rebuilding operations, future business activity and tourism, and it's clear that talk of $100 billion, with a 20 percent swing factor, is little more than inspired guessing. The federal government's aid package totals $21.5 billion, with $2.75 billion of it for WTC site and area clean-up, and $1.8 billion for subway system repair. Capital costs for a rebuilt transportation hub alone top $7 billion—but in part would fund expanded facilities. Only after below-surface infrastructure is completed can new buildings arise, their costs yet unknown.

At best, redevelopment of the WTC site will prove to be a catalyst for greatly increased economic activity throughout Lower Manhattan. Paradoxically, the greatest long-term costs may accrue to non-allied nations for whom agricultural, industrial, transportation, communications and scientific technologies (the tools of 21st-century progress) are transfers from the West, paid for in oil—whose value decreases as additional oil-producing regions enter the market.

154-155
A grieving father looks down from the Family Room to Ground Zero, where his firefighter son lost his life in the rescue operations.

160 AND 161
"TRIBUTE IN LIGHT" DRAMATICALLY
COMMEMORATED THE SIX-MONTH
ANNIVERSARY OF 9/11. FOR MILLIONS IT
ALSO SIGNALED CONFIDENCE IN NEW YORK
AND ITS FUTURE.

6

REBUILDING THE WTC

On February 27, 2003 the Lower Manhattan Development Corporation (LMDC) selected Studio Daniel Libeskind's "Memory Foundations" design to shape redevelopment of the WTC. In commemorating tragedy, this dramatic vision also projects belief in a transcendent future.

The design process was daunting. Participating firms had to accommodate to the reconstruction of subterranean subway, rail, and electrical distribution systems, and repair of the "bathtub," the WTC basement's 7-story water-excluding wall. Equally challenging were the competing priorities of the Port Authority (the site owner), the operating company, hundreds of displaced businesses, and the LMDC--the State-City body charged with managing redevelopment of the 16-acre site. The families of the deceased expressed heartfelt expectations: creation within the bathtub of a memorial to 9/11 victims, a park, and cultural/performing arts centers in much of the immense area. The need to respond to these non-commercial expectations clearly influenced the seven finalists' designs.

Above ground, New Yorkers favored reinstitution of the historic street grid and traditional human activity, not just gigantic office towers. A multipurpose environment in which cultural endeavors flourished was more important than a restored business dynamo.

Pragmatism tempered by sensibility drove the LMDC to select the Memory Foundations design over the Rafael Viñoly/THINK team's World Cultural Center design, with its high-appeal twin lattice towers. The Memory Foundations design preserves the Twin Towers' footprints; it treats the entire bathtub as a commemorative site, incorporating Heroes Park, a memorial, and retaining a raw bathtub wall. Overhead, a cantilevered, glass-walled museum will interpret 9/11's many dimensions and serve as a formal entry. Above ground, a 1,776 ft glass spire enclosing gardens symbolizing life will rise, while an elevated site-encircling promenade will provide panoramic views of Heroes Park and the memorial. Office tower locations are planned to allow a "Wedge of Light" to illuminate the site on 9/11, from first impact to second collapse.

The Memorial Foundations design had no easy birth; rather, it evolved through the LMDC's demanding process. Recognizing numerous constituencies--families of the dead, major corporations, small businesses, civic organizations, and local residents -- the LMDC adopted a redevelopment design process of maximum openness.

162 TOP
PAOLO SOLERI'S "SECULAR CATHEDRAL": ROOTED IN RENAISSANCE HUMANISM, THE EMBRACING STRUCTURE IS DESIGNED TO SERVE THE WHOLE COMMUNITY.

162-163
"THE WORLD FORUM" -- PART-MEMORIAL, PART-OFFICE AND CULTURAL CENTER -- AND "THE WORLD BRIDGE," A GRACEFUL, PEDESTRIANS-ONLY SPAN LINKING NEW YORK AND NEW JERSEY. EYTAN KAUFMAN DESIGN AND DEVELOPMENT.

163 BOTTOM
NOX ARCHITEKTEN PROPOSES A SEEMINGLY WHIMSICAL TOP-DOWN DESIGN THAT DRAWS UPON THE "WOOL THREAD" CONCEPT OF OTTO FREI.

In July 2002, six redevelopment concepts (from over 400 submissions) were exhibited. Public response was negative: the designs lacked vision; they favored office towers over an inspiring memorial. Seeking broader public input, the LMDC involved over 5,000 participants. Modified criteria were issued; commercial space was reduced. A panel of architectural experts then invited seven prestigious firms to submit "innovative designs" to reflect strongly voiced public and private concerns. In December 2002 nine designs were exhibited in the Winter Garden, adjoining the WTC site. More than 100,000 people viewed the models; some 8000 submitted comments, and additional thousands commented via other media. The Memory Foundations design, backed by Governor George Pataki and Mayor Michael Bloomberg, garnered substantial public support, particularly for its Heroes Park and "Wedge of Light" concept. The design persuasively addressed underground transportation needs, restored the street grid, and provided for future medium-height office towers while re-integrating the WTC area into Lower Manhattan, itself the focus of an ambitious redevelopment plan. Building the iconic 1,776 ft spire has become an announced public priority, a powerful commitment that a dazzling WTC will triumphantly rise, worthy of those lost and those who commemorate them.

164-165
THE STUDIO LIBESKIND MEMORIAL FOUNDATIONS DESIGN, LOOKING NORTH TO THE 1,776 FT ICONIC SPIRE. HEROES PARK AND A MEMORIAL WILL OCCUPY THE BELOW-GRADE GROUND ZERO, ENDING UNDER THE CANTILEVERED MUSEUM AND GLASS-CLAD WALL. AT LEFT, THE "RAW" BATHTUB WALL WILL BE RETAINED. ENCIRCLING THE SITE IS A RAISED PEDESTRIAN WALKWAY SEEN ABOVE A PROPOSED "GRAND AVENUE" WEST STREET.

165
THE TORCH OF LIBERTY GREETS THE MEMORIAL FOUNDATIONS' 1,776 FT SPIRE, RECALLING THE AMERICAN REVOLUTION AND THE BIRTH OF THE NATION'S FREEDOM.

166-167 AND 166 BOTTOM
GROUND ZERO FROM WEST: THE ORANGE-TONED PUBLIC ENTRY HALL, THE ROOF OF THE CANTILEVERED MUSEUM AND, LEFT, THE PROPOSED CULTURAL/PERFORMING ARTS CENTER. SMALLER TOWERS AND NUMEROUS TREES WILL HELP TO OPEN AND LIGHT THE AREA.

CHAPTER

6

THE CHALLENGE OF THE FUTURE

CREDITS

The Publisher would like to thank:
The New York Times
The Skyscraper Museum of New York
Minoru Yamasaki Associates
Veronica Di Nardo and Piero Piccardi, World Trade Center Association - Rome
Carmen Figini, Archivio Editoriale Domus
Fabio Grazioli
All the pictures courtesy of Max Protetch Gallery, are from the book A New World Trade Center, *published by Regan Books in August 2002.*

The author is deeply grateful to Mike Wallace for generous encouragement.

Translation of chapter "The Twin Towers: design and architecture" by CTM, Milan.

EDITORIAL COORDINATION:
LAURA ACCOMAZZO, MARIA VALERIA URBANI GRECCHI, CLAUDIA ZANERA

ALL CAPTIONS EXCEPT CHAPTER TWO BY PETER SKINNER